Excel

A Comprehensive Guide to the Basics, Formulas, Functions, Charts, and Tables in Excel with Step-by-Step Instructions and Practical Examples

Adam K. Grubb

ISBN-13: 979-8872359531

DEDICATION

To every one of my readers!

TABLE OF CONTENT

Introduction

Microsoft Excel is a powerful and widely used spreadsheet program that allows users to organize, analyze, and visualize data. Whether you're a student, a professional, or simply someone looking to manage personal finances, Excel offers a range of features and functions that can help streamline your tasks and improve your productivity.

One of Excel's key strengths is its ability to handle large amounts of data with ease. You can input data into cells, which are organized into columns and rows, and then perform calculations, create charts, and generate reports based on that data. With Excel, you can easily manipulate and analyze your data, making it a valuable tool for tasks such as budgeting, financial analysis, and data tracking.

Excel also provides a wide variety of functions that allow you to perform complex calculations and automate repetitive tasks. Functions like SUM, AVERAGE, and COUNT help you quickly calculate totals, averages, and counts of data, while functions like IF and VLOOKUP allow you to perform logical and lookup operations. By using functions, you can save time and ensure accuracy in your calculations.

In addition to its data manipulation capabilities, Excel offers a range of formatting options that allow you to present your data in a visually appealing and easy-to-understand manner. You can apply different fonts, colors, borders, and number formats to your cells, as well as create charts and graphs to visualize your data. Excel also provides conditional formatting, which allows you to highlight cells based on specific criteria, making it easier to identify trends and patterns in your data.

Collaboration is another key feature of Excel. Multiple users can work on the same spreadsheet simultaneously, making it a great tool for team projects and data sharing. Excel also allows you to protect your data by setting permissions and passwords, ensuring that only authorized individuals can make changes to the spreadsheet.

In conclusion, Microsoft Excel is a versatile and powerful tool for data management and analysis. Its user-friendly interface, extensive range of functions, and formatting options make it accessible to users of all skill levels. Whether you're crunching numbers, creating charts, or collaborating with others, Excel provides the tools you need to automate your tasks and make better-informed decisions. So, why not explore the possibilities of Excel and unlock its potential for your personal and professional endeavors?

Chapter 1: Microsoft Excel Fundamentals

MS Excel, a software that comes with the Microsoft Office suite, is an electronic spreadsheet that arranges data in rows and columns. Users can organize data, create visual representations, and perform calculations using this program. With 1,048,576 rows and 16,384 columns, each cell is identified by a combination of column name and row number (e.g., A1, D2). This is commonly referred to as a cell reference.

1.1 What is Microsoft Excel?

MS Excel is a software program developed by Microsoft that allows users to create and manage data tables. With its intuitive interface, it simplifies the process of inputting and organizing data. What's more? It offers a convenient way to analyze and manipulate data effectively.

1.2 What is a Cell?

To put it simply, a cell is the basic unit of a spreadsheet. It is formed at the point where a row and a column meet, resulting in a rectangular box. Much like a table, a spreadsheet is made up of rows and columns, and cells are created at their intersections. Cells are essential for organizing and manipulating data in a spreadsheet, and they often contain numerical or text-based information.

1.3 Understanding Cell Reference or Address?

In Excel, a cell reference, also known as a cell address or cell name, is the identification of a specific cell or range of cells. It allows Excel to locate the cell and retrieve the data or value needed for a formula. Cell references can be used to reference cells on other worksheets as well.

In Excel, there are three main types of cell references:

1.3.1 Absolute Reference

This type of reference remains fixed, regardless of where the formula is copied or moved. It is denoted by the dollar sign ($) before the column letter and row number (e.g., A1).

1.3.2 Relative Reference

A relative reference adjusts according to the position of the formula when it is copied or moved to another cell. It does not contain any dollar signs. For example, if a formula refers to cell A1 and is copied to cell B2, the reference will automatically change to B2.

1.3.3 Mixed Reference

A mixed reference is a combination of absolute and relative references. Either the column or row reference is fixed using the dollar sign. For instance, $A1 will keep the column constant but adjust the row when copied, while A$1 will keep the row constant but adjust the column.

1.4 Getting Accustomed with Excel's Ribbon

The Excel Ribbon is the row of tabs located at the top of the interface that offers various functions and features to users. These tabs include:

1.4.1 The Home Tab

The Home tab in Excel is where you'll find essential features for formatting your spreadsheet. Here, you can easily customize the font, adjust text size, and make edits to cells. You can also take advantage of convenient tools like Autosum, which simplifies the process of adding up numbers in your spreadsheet. This tab is a go-to for many users, as it offers a range of useful functions to enhance your Excel experience.

1.4.2 The Insert Tab

The Insert tab in Excel offers various features for adding links, charts, clip art, images, pivot tables, tables, and more. It allows users to enhance their spreadsheets by easily incorporating these elements. By utilizing the functionalities found in the Insert tab, Excel users can efficiently enrich their data and present it in a visually appealing manner. Whether it's inserting hyperlinks to external resources, visualizing data through charts, or incorporating images to enhance the overall presentation, the Insert tab provides a range of tools to enhance the user experience and improve data analysis capabilities.

1.4.3 The Page Layout Tab

The Page Layout tab in Excel offers a range of features that allow you to customize the look and feel of your spreadsheet. You can adjust elements such as the background, width, height, orientation, and margins. This ensures that the appearance of your worksheet remains consistent when printed out. By utilizing the Page Layout tab, you have greater control over the visual presentation of your data in both digital and hard copy formats.

1.4.4 The Formulas Tab

The Formulas tab in Excel contains a variety of built-in formulas and functions that users can utilize simply by selecting the desired cells or cell range. These formulas and functions help perform calculations and manipulate data within the spreadsheet. By accessing the Formulas tab, users can easily access and apply these pre-built formulas to streamline their data analysis and mathematical operations, providing a convenient and efficient way to work with values in Excel.

1.4.5 The Data Tab

Excel's Data Tab is a useful feature that allows users to perform various tasks on large sets of data. With this tab, you can analyze your data using tools like what-if analysis and other data analysis tools. You can also transpose columns and rows, get rid of duplicate data, and access data from different sources, such as on the web or via Microsoft Access. This tab provides a range of functions to help you work with your data more efficiently.

1.4.6 The Review Tab

Microsoft Excel's Review tab offers a range of helpful features to enhance your experience. With this tab, you can effortlessly find synonyms using the thesaurus, translate text into different languages, ensure accurate spelling, and safeguard and distribute your workbook and worksheet. This comprehensive array of tools empowers users to optimize their work and collaborate seamlessly.

1.4.7 The View Tab

The View Tab in Excel consists of various commands that allow users to control the display of the workbook. These commands include options to show or hide gridlines, rulers, and other elements. Additionally, users can add macros and freeze panes through this tab. By utilizing the View Tab, users can customize their Excel experience and optimize their workflow.

1.5 How to Add a New Excel Spreadsheet

You will find three automatically opened sheets in Excel. If you would like to add a new sheet, follow these steps:

- Locate the button in the bottom pane of Excel.
- Create a new sheet by clicking on the button.
- Alternatively, you can right-click on the sheet number where you would like to add the new sheet.
- From the options that appear, choose "Insert."
- Click on "Worksheet."
- Hit "OK" to complete the process.

1.6 Opening a Pre-existing Worksheet

- At the bottom of the Excel window, you'll find the name of the currently active sheet.
- You'll see the names of previous sheets, such as Sheet 2, 3, or 4, on the left side of this sheet. To open a specific sheet, click on its corresponding name or number.
- For instance, if you're currently on Sheet 5 and would like to access Sheet 3, you should click on Sheet 3, and it will open within the same workbook.

1.7 Saving the Workbook

- Navigate to the File tab or click on the Office button.

- Select the Save As option.
- Enter the desired name for your file.
- Click OK to save.

1.8 Sharing Your Workbook

To share your workbook, follow these steps:

- Locate the ribbon and select the Review tab.
- Locate the Changes group and click on the Share Workbook option.
- Select the Protect and Share Workbook option if you would like to safeguard your workbook and make it accessible to someone else.
- In the Share Workbook dialog box, tick the box that says "Allow changes by more than one user at the same time. This also allows workbook merging."
- You can explore additional options in the Advanced section, such as tracking and updating changes.
- Finally, click OK to proceed with the sharing process.

Chapter 2: Working with Excel Workbooks

2.1 Renaming a Worksheet

Excel automatically assigns names to its worksheets in a numerical sequence, starting with Sheet1, Sheet2, Sheet3, etc. However, renaming them can be easy, and you can do it in three different ways:

- Locate the specific sheet tab that you would like to rename, right-click on it, select Rename, and enter the new name.
- Locate the specific sheet tab that you would like to rename, double-click it, and enter the new name.
- Press the keys Alt+H > O > R on your keyboard, and enter the new name.

Note: It is crucial to choose appropriate names for worksheets. Here are some guidelines to keep in mind:

- Worksheet names should not be left blank.
- Avoid using certain characters such as / \ ? * : [ ] in the names.
- Keep the name within 31 characters.
- Avoid starting or ending the name with an apostrophe ('), although it can be used within the name.
- For instance, the name "02/17/2016" would not be valid, but "02-17-2016" would be acceptable.
- Do not use the name "History," as it is reserved for internal use by Excel.

2.2 Renaming Your Workbook

Renaming a workbook is a simple task that can be done in just a few steps.

- To get started, find the workbook in Windows Explorer.
- Once you've found it, you can either hit the F2 key on your keyboard or right-click on the file and choose "Rename."
- Enter the new name you would like for the workbook, and you're good to go.

If you have the workbook open already, you can still rename it.

- Navigate to the "File" tab and select "Save As." This is going to make a duplicate of the current workbook with the name you choose.

2.3 Inserting a Worksheet

To add a new worksheet to your workbook, you have a couple of options.

- You can click on the plus icon labeled "New Sheet," located at the bottom of the workbook.
- Alternatively, you can go to the "Home" tab, click on "Insert," and then select "Insert Sheet."

Both methods will allow you to easily insert a new worksheet into your workbook.

2.4 Moving a Worksheet

Moving a worksheet is a simple task in Excel.

- To relocate a worksheet to the end, you can right-click on the sheet tab, select "Move or Copy," choose "Move to End" from the options, and click "OK."
- Alternatively, you can click on the sheet tab and drag to the desired position within the workbook.

2.5 Deleting a Worksheet

Deleting a worksheet in Excel is a straightforward process. You have two options to delete a worksheet.

- The first method is to right-click on the sheet tab and choose the "Delete" option from the context menu.
- The second method is to select the sheet, go to the "Home" tab, click on "Delete," and then select "Delete Sheet."

2.6 Changing a Sheet Tab's Background Fill Color

If you want to enhance the visibility of your sheet tabs in Excel, one way to do so is by adding a background fill color. This simple formatting change can make a significant difference. However, it's important to note that Excel doesn't provide options for changing the font color, size, or style on a sheet tab.

To change the color of a sheet tab, follow these steps:

- Right-click on the tab you want to modify.
- From the context menu, select "Tab Color."
- Choose the desired color from the available options.

Recommendation: To view the updated tab color, click away from the styled tab.

Note: If you wish to get rid of the color, repeat the process, but select "No Color" instead.

2.7 How to Switch Between Worksheets

When you first open an Excel workbook, you'll see the default sheet. But what if you have multiple worksheets and need to switch between them? Don't worry, it's easy! Just follow these simple steps:

- Locate the worksheet tabs. They're located above the status bar at the bottom of your Excel window.
- Hover your mouse pointer over the tab of the worksheet you want to switch to. You'll notice that the tab becomes bold, indicating that it's selected.
- Click on the tab. This will open the selected worksheet, which is now referred to as the "active sheet."
- Sometimes, you may have hidden sheets that aren't visible. To reveal them, click on the arrow next to the first displayed sheet's tab. Then, select the sheet you want to show.

2.7.1 Switching between Non-Adjacent Sheets

When it comes to switching between your worksheets, the previous technique mentioned might be simple enough. However, things can get a bit bewildering if you have numerous sheets or if some of them are hidden. Additionally, it can become quite frustrating if you constantly have to click back and forth between sheets.

To address this issue, you can employ an alternative method to switch between your Excel worksheets:

If you need to navigate swiftly between non-adjacent sheets, you can utilize the Ctrl + Shift + Page Up or Ctrl + Shift + Page Down shortcuts. This handy shortcut enables you to easily transition to the previous or next sheet, irrespective of its location within the workbook.

2.8 Grouping and Ungrouping Worksheets

Performing tasks on multiple worksheets simultaneously becomes easy when you group them together. By grouping worksheets, any changes made on one worksheet will be replicated on all other worksheets in the group at the same location. This feature can be particularly useful when creating standard tables or calculations on a large number of worksheets, saving you valuable time. However, it works best when the worksheets already have similar data structures.

2.8.1 Grouping Selected Worksheets

Imagine a scenario where you have a workbook containing various worksheets representing different cities. Each worksheet follows the same format, displaying sales data for coffee drinks.

If you're looking to accomplish identical tasks across multiple worksheets, here are some straightforward steps to follow:

- To simultaneously select multiple worksheet tabs, simply click on the tabs you wish to group while holding down the Ctrl key. If the tabs you would like to group are consecutive, you can click the first tab, hold down the Shift key, and click on the last tab to select them all at once.
- Now, let's say you want to apply the same formula to cell C8 on the worksheets labeled "London" and "Paris." By grouping these worksheets, any changes made to the formula on one worksheet will automatically be applied to the other.

Please note that the workbook's name turns into [Group] after you group the worksheets.

2.8.2 Grouping All Worksheets

To group every worksheet in a workbook, simply follow these steps:

- Begin by right-clicking on any worksheet tab.
- Next, click on the option labeled "Select All Sheets.".

It's important to note that grouping all the worksheets causes them to become ungrouped when you browse through them. If you refrain from selecting all worksheets, you may still look through the group of worksheets without being forced to automatically ungroup them.

2.8.3 Ungrouping Selected Worksheets

Worksheets can be ungrouped if you choose not to apply particular tasks to a certain group of worksheets.

- To ungroup the specific worksheet tabs, press and hold the Ctrl key while clicking on the intended tab(s).

2.8.4 Ungrouping All Worksheets

Once you've completed your modifications, you can proceed to ungroup the worksheets in a few simple steps.

- Start by right-clicking on any worksheet tab that is part of the group.
- Then, select the option to ungroup sheets.
- Alternatively, you can simply click on any worksheet tab that is not part of the group to ungroup all the worksheets.

2.9 Using the Page Layout View

The Page Layout View is a useful feature that allows you to preview how your document will look when printed. It helps you make easy adjustments to ensure that your pages are perfectly aligned. In this section, we will show you how to use the page layout view in Excel to improve the way your data is presented and enhance the overall look of your document. By following these steps, you can gain better control over the appearance of your document and make it more visually appealing.

2.9.1 How Does the Page Layout View Work?

Excel's Page Layout View is one of the main worksheet views available. Its purpose is to provide a clear and organized layout by dividing the worksheet into separate pages. This view gives you a comprehensive look at the page layout, including margins, headers, and footers. With Page Layout View, you can:

- Add and customize headers and footers.
- Quickly spot page breaks.
- Get a complete print preview, allowing you to see how the final printed page will look.
- Adjust margins easily using the gray boxes on the ruler.

2.9.2 How Can Page Layout View Be Used?

The page layout view can be accessed in two ways, which are as follows:

2.9.2.1 Using Excel's View Tab

To use Excel's view tab to access the page layout view, follow these steps:

- Open an Excel file on your computer.
- Proceed to the top of your screen and look for the "View" tab.
- Click on "Page Layout" in the Excel ribbon, which is located next to the "Page Break Preview" option.
- Your page will resemble physical papers in this view, appearing as sheets. This gives you a preview of what your information will look like after printing.
- Use the ruler to make precise adjustments to the page settings and layout.
- You can also further customize the view by hiding the gridlines, formula bar, and rulers according to your preferences.
- To switch back to the regular view of the Excel spreadsheet, simply click on the "Normal" option.

This method offers a straightforward and convenient approach to accessing the page layout view in Excel. It allows for quick and efficient adjustments, particularly useful when making last-minute changes before printing a document.

2.9.2.2 Using the Page Layout View Button

- To access the Page Layout View in Excel, simply click on the small button located at the lower-right corner. This will switch your view to the page layout mode.
- To return to the normal view, click on the Normal View button next to the Page Layout View option in Excel.

Chapter 3: Data Management in Excel

3.1 Modifying Data (Cell Content)

When you want to modify the data in a cell, there are two ways to do it: by double-clicking the cell or by using the Formula Bar. As you type data into a cell, you'll see it simultaneously appear in the formula bar. This bar serves the purpose of both inputting data into cells and editing existing data. Entering and editing data in a cell location can be done by following these steps:

- Start by selecting the desired cell (e.g., A2) in the worksheet.
- Enter the abbreviation "Tot" and hit the ENTER key.
- Click on cell A2 again.
- Point the mouse cursor upward toward the formula bar. The pointer will change to a cursor. Left-click after moving the cursor to the end of the letters "Tot."
- Enter the final letter "al" in order to create the word "Total."
- To confirm the change, click on the checkmark located to the left of the formula bar.
- Double-click on cell A2.
- After "Total," insert a space and enter the word "Sales."
- Hit the Enter key on your keyboard to finalize the edit.

Pro Tip: If you would like to use keyboard shortcuts to modify a cell's data, select it and simply press the F2 key on your keyboard. This shortcut allows for quick and efficient editing without the need for extensive mouse navigation.

3.2 Removing Data and Formatting from Cells

To eliminate the content within cells, such as comments, formats (which include borders, conditional formats, and number formats), data, and formulas, you have the option to clear them. By doing so, the cells will be left empty or without any formatting on the worksheet.

To remove data from specific columns, rows, or cells in Excel, follow these steps:

- Select the columns, rows, or cells you wish to clear. Tip: You can click any cell on the worksheet to undo the selection of cells that you have made.
- Proceed to the Home tab, locate the Editing group, find the Clear button, and click on the arrow beside it. From there, you have several options:

    a) Clear All: This option will remove all contents, comments, and formats within the selected cells.
    b) Clear Formats: Selecting this option will only clear the formatting applied to the selected cells.

c) Clear Contents: This option will clear the actual data within the selected cells while preserving any comments and formats.
d) Clear Comments and Notes: If there are any notes or comments attached to the cells that were selected, this option will get rid of them.
e) Clear Hyperlinks: Choose this option to clear any hyperlinks associated with the selected cells.

3.3 Copying or Moving Cells and Cell Contents

Copying and moving cell contents in Excel can be done easily using Cut, Copy, and Paste. These functions allow you to copy or move specific contents or attributes from cells. For instance, you can copy the value of a formula without copying the formula itself, or you can copy only the formula.

When a cell is copied or moved, Excel ensures that all the necessary elements are copied or moved as well. This includes formulas and their resulting values, any comments, and cell formats attached to the cell.

To move cells in Excel, you can either drag and drop them or use the Cut and Paste commands. These simple techniques make rearranging your data a breeze.

3.3.1 Using Cut and Paste to Move Cells

To use the cut-and-paste feature to move cells in Excel, follow these simple steps:

- Choose the desired cell or range of cells.

- Click on the "Cut" option located in the "Home" tab, or use the shortcut Ctrl + X.
- Select the destination cell where you would like to move the data.
- Click on the "Paste" option in the "Home" tab or use the shortcut Ctrl + V.

3.3.2 Dragging and Dropping Cells

- To move cells through drag and drop:
- Select the cells or range of cells you wish to copy or move.
- Hover over the edge of the selection.
- Once the cursor transforms into a moving icon, simply drag the cell or range of cells to a new position.

3.3.3 Using Copy and Paste to Copy Cells

Copying cells in Excel is a simple process.

- To do this, first, select the cell or range of cells you want to copy.
- Next, either click on the "Copy" option or use the shortcut Ctrl + C on your keyboard.
- Finally, select the "Paste" option or use the shortcut Ctrl + V to complete the copying process.

3.4 Using Excel's Fill Handle for Easier Data Entry

The fill handle is a useful tool in Excel that allows you to quickly copy and paste or reference values.

- To use it, simply select the initial value you want to duplicate, then drag the fill handle across or down the spreadsheet while holding the right mouse button.
- Release the button when you reach the end of your data. This allows you to easily replicate values without having to manually input them one by one.

3.5 Adjusting the Row Height and Column Width in Excel

To modify the height of a row or the width of a column, you have the option to do it manually or allow the spreadsheet to adjust them automatically based on the data. Remember that the boundary refers to the line that separates rows, columns, and cells. In the event that a column is too small to show the data, you'll notice the appearance of ### in the cell.

3.5.1 Resizing the Columns

When it comes to adjusting column sizes in Excel, the process is fairly straightforward. Here's a step-by-step guide:

- First, choose the column or range of columns that you want to resize.
- On the Home tab, locate the Format option and click on it.
- From the drop-down menu, select either column width or column height, depending on your specific needs.
- A dialog box will appear, allowing you to enter the desired width or height for the selected column(s).
- Once you've entered the value, click on the OK button to finalize the changes.

3.5.2 Resizing the Rows

Resizing rows in Excel is a simple task. Here's how you can do it:

- First, select the row or rows that you want to resize.
- Next, go to the Home tab and click on Format.
- From the drop-down menu, select either row width or row height, depending on your preference.

- A dialog box will appear where you can enter the desired size for the row. Type in the value and click OK.

3.5.3 Automatically Resizing Every Row and Column to Accommodate the Data

To automatically adjust the size of rows and columns to accommodate your data, follow these steps:

- Click on the "Select All" button located at the topmost section of the worksheet. This will highlight all the rows and columns.
- Double-click on any of the boundaries between rows or columns. This action will automatically resize them to match the size of the data they contain.

3.6 Cell Formatting

In Excel, you have the option to format individual cells or groups of cells. This allows you to customize the appearance of your data. To put it simply, the cells act as a frame, while the data inside the cells is like the picture within that frame. So, you can apply formatting to the frame itself or to the picture within it, depending on your needs.

3.6.1 Formatting Cells

How to Format Cells in Excel:

- Begin by selecting the cells that you want to format.
- Navigate to the ribbon menu, where you can find various formatting options like bold, font color, and font size.
- Choose the desired formatting option to apply it to the selected cells.

3.6.2 Applying Excel Styles

If you want to apply styles to your cells or data in Excel, here's how you can do it:

- Choose the cells you want to style.
- Go to the Home tab and click on Cell Style.
- From the options, select a style that suits your needs.

3.6.3 Modifying an Excel Style

If you would like to modify an Excel style, do the following:

- Choose the cells that have the Excel style applied.

- Right-click on the style in the "Home" tab under "Cell Styles."
- Click on "Modify" and then select "Format" to make the desired changes.

3.7 Conditional Formatting

In Excel, you can use conditional formatting to alter the visual appearance of cells within a selected range. By setting up rules based on matching text or specific numerical values, you can effectively highlight important data points for analysis. This feature allows you to change the colors, fonts, and other formatting elements of cells, making it easier to identify and interpret relevant information.

In the online version of Excel, you have a limited number of preset options for conditional formatting. However, if you use the Excel application, you can create personalized conditional formatting rules to meet your specific needs. This gives you a lot more flexibility and control over how your data is formatted based on certain conditions. So, if you want to have more freedom in formatting your data, it's worth using the Excel application rather than the web browser version.

3.7.1 Applying Conditional Formatting

To illustrate, suppose you want to determine the speed values of different Pokémon using color-scale conditional formatting. Imagine you have a column that contains Pokémon characters and another column that lists their respective speeds, like Wartortle 57, Squirtle 42, Charizard 100, Charmeleon 81, Charmander 64, Venusaur 81, Ivysaur 62, and Bulbasaur 46.

Here's a simple guide to using conditional formatting:

- Choose the range of speed values you want to work with (for example, C2:C9).
- Look for the Conditional Formatting icon in the Home menu ribbon and click on it.
- From the options that appear, select Color Scales.

You have a choice of 12 color scale options, each offering a unique range of colors. The color that appears at the top of the icon will be applied to the highest values.

- To select the "Green, Yellow, and Red Color Scale" option, simply click on the corresponding icon.

The speed value cells will be visually emphasized with different background colors. The cells with the highest values will be highlighted in dark green, while the cells with the lowest values will be highlighted in dark red. For instance, Charizard will have the highest speed value, which is 100, while Squirtle will have the lowest speed value, which is 42. The background colors of the cells in the range will gradually transition from green, to yellow, to orange, and finally to red.

3.8 Cell Merging and Text Wrapping

When text exceeds the size of a cell, the spreadsheet offers the option to wrap the text, allowing it to appear on multiple lines within the cell. Alternatively, you can merge cells, joining more than one neighboring cell into a single, larger cell.

3.8.1 Text Wrapping in a Cell

To make text wrap within a cell, follow these steps:

- Choose a cell or a group of cells that contain the text you would like to wrap.
- Go to the Home tab and find the Alignment group.
- Click on the Wrap Text button. This will cause the text to appear on multiple lines in the cell.

- If you want to revert to the original display, simply click the Wrap Text button again. The text will go back to its original format before wrapping was applied.

3.8.2 Cell Merging

To merge cells, simply follow these steps:

- Choose the cells you would like to merge. Important: To merge cells in Excel, ensure that the information you want to display in the merged cell is located in the top-left cell of the range you selected. Only the content of this cell will be preserved in the merged cell, while the data in the other cells will be erased.
- To combine cells and align text in a merged cell, go to the Home tab and proceed to the Alignment section. Click on the drop-down arrow next to the Merge Cells button and choose one of the options below:

  a) Merge & Center: merges the selected cells and centers the text in the merged cell.
  b) Merge Cells: merges the selected cells into a single cell.
  c) Merge Across: merges the rows of the selected cell range into larger cells.

- In case you have a change of heart and decide to separate a merged cell, simply choose the desired cell and click on the "Unmerge Cells" option found in the drop-down menu of the "Merge Cells" button. By doing so, the information from the merged cell will be displayed in the top-left cell of the split cell range.

3.9 Show or Hide Columns

Simplify your spreadsheet experience by concealing or revealing specific columns. This allows you to focus solely on the relevant data for viewing or printing purposes.

3.9.1 Hiding Columns

To conceal columns in Excel, follow these steps:

- Choose the desired columns by clicking to select them. To select non-adjacent columns, press the Ctrl key while clicking.
- Next, right-click on the highlighted columns and choose the "Hide" option.

Remember: If you see a double line between two columns, it means that you have successfully concealed a column.

3.9.2 Unhiding Columns

If you want to reveal columns that are currently hidden in Excel, follow these steps:

- Choose the columns on either side of the hidden ones that you wish to unhide.
- Right-click the selected columns and choose the "Unhide" option.
- Alternatively, you can double-click on the line between the two adjacent columns where the hidden columns are located. This will automatically unhide them.

3.10 Inserting or Deleting Columns and Rows

Improve the organization of your worksheet by adding or removing columns and rows. Please be aware that Microsoft Excel has certain limitations in terms of the number of columns (16,384) and rows (1,048,576) it can accommodate.

3.10.1 Inserting or Deleting a Row

To add or remove a row in Excel, follow these steps:

- First, choose a cell within the row you would like to modify.
- Next, navigate to the Home tab and click on the Insert button. From the drop-down menu, select "Insert Sheet Rows" to add a row, or "Delete Sheet Rows" to remove a row.
- Another method is to right-click on the row number and choose either "Insert" or "Delete" from the context menu.

3.10.2 Inserting or Deleting a Column

To add or remove a column in Excel, follow these steps:

- Choose a cell within the column you want to modify.

- Navigate to the Home tab and click on Insert. From the drop-down menu, select Insert Sheet Columns to add a column or Delete Sheet Columns to remove a column.
- Another way to accomplish this is by right-clicking on the top of the column. A context menu will appear, and you can choose either Insert or Delete to make the necessary changes.

3.10.3 Formatting Options

The formatting that was previously applied to a column or row when you selected it will be replicated in each of the new columns or rows that you create. After inserting, you may click the Insert options button and select one of the following choices if you wish to forego the formatting:

- Format Same as Right
- Format Same as Left
- Clear Formatting

If you can't see the Insert Options button, follow these steps: Go to the File menu, select Options, then choose Advanced. In the Cut, copy, and paste group, make sure to select the option that says Show Insert Options button.

3.11 Transposing or Rotating Data from Columns to Rows and Vice Versa

Imagine you've got a worksheet full of data organized neatly in rows, but you need it in columns instead. No worries! There's a handy feature called Transpose that can help you with that. It allows you to effortlessly switch data from rows to columns, or vice versa.

Note: You won't find the Transpose feature if you have data in an Excel table. However, there's an alternative you can try. You can convert the table into a range and then use the Transpose feature.

Let's see how it's done:

- First, select the range of data you would like to rearrange, along with any column or row labels. Press Ctrl+C to copy the data. Remember, using Ctrl+X or the Cut command won't work for this task.
- Next, find a suitable location in your worksheet where you would like to paste the transposed table. Make sure there is enough space to accommodate your data. Keep in mind that the new table will overwrite any existing data or formatting in that area.

- Right-click on the top-left cell of the desired paste location. Look for the Transpose button in the options that appear. Click on it to transpose the data.
- Once the data is successfully rotated, you can safely delete the initial table. The data in the transposed table will not change.

3.11.1 Tips on Transposing Data

- When working with data in Excel, it's important to ensure that any formulas you have included are updated correctly when you move or rotate the data. Excel does this automatically, but it's always a good idea to double-check. If you find that your formulas are not updating correctly, you can switch between relative, absolute, and mixed references to fix the issue before rotating the data.
- If you frequently need to view your data from different angles, you might want to consider creating a pivot table. This allows you to easily pivot your data by dragging fields from the Rows area to the Columns area (or vice versa) in the PivotTable Field List. This can be a handy way to quickly analyze and manipulate your data from various perspectives.

3.12 Validating Data in Cells

One way to control the type of data or values that users enter into a cell is by using data validation. This feature allows you to limit the options available to users, such as creating a drop-down list. When you implement data validation, you can ensure that only appropriate and valid data is entered into the cell, improving the accuracy and reliability of your spreadsheet.

To validate your data, follow these steps:

- Choose the cell or cells where you would like to set your data validation rule.
- Proceed to the Data tab and select Data Validation.
- Under Allow in the Settings tab, choose from the following options:

Decimal: Restricts the cell to accept only decimal numbers.

Whole Number: Allows only whole numbers in the cell.

List: Creates a drop-down list for selecting data.

Time: Limits the cell to accepting only time values.

Date: Limits the cell to accepting only dates.

Text Length: Sets a maximum length for the text in the cell.

Custom: Allows you to create a custom formula.

- Select the condition that you want to apply under Data.
- Set the necessary values based on the options you chose.
- Customize the Input Message tab to provide instructions to users.
- Check the "Show input message when cell is selected" box to show the instructions when the user interacts with the cell or cells.
- Customize the Error Alert tab to create an error text and choose a style.
- Click OK to apply the data validation.

In the event that the user inputs an invalid value, an error alert will be triggered, displaying a personalized message.

3.13 Using Excel's Flash Fill Feature

Automated data filling is a convenient feature offered by Flash Fill. By detecting patterns in your data, it can effortlessly split first and last names from a single column or merge them from separate columns. It's important to note that Flash Fill is exclusively available in Excel 2013 onwards.

Imagine you have a spreadsheet with a column for first names (X) and another for last names (Y), and you want to create a new column (Z) where you can combine the first and last names. Excel's Flash Fill feature can help you achieve this. By manually typing the full name in the first row of column Z, Excel will analyze the pattern and automatically fill in the remaining cells based on that pattern. This saves you time and effort by automating the process for you.

- In cell Z2, input the complete name and use the ENTER key.
- Proceed to enter the subsequent full name in cell Z3. Excel will detect the pattern you establish and display a preview of the remaining column filled with the combined text.
- To confirm the preview, use the ENTER key.

3.13.1 Turning on Flash Fill's Preview

If the preview doesn't appear when using Flash Fill, it could be because it's not enabled.

- To manually run Flash Fill, you can navigate to the Data tab and select Flash Fill, or simply press Ctrl+E.
- To enable Flash Fill, go to the Tools menu, choose Options, then select Advanced. Under Editing Options, make sure to check the box that says "Automatically Flash Fill."

3.14 Using the Quick Analysis Tool for Instant Charts

Quick Analysis is a tool that simplifies the process of choosing the right chart for your data. Here's a step-by-step guide:

- First, choose the range of cells containing your data.
- Look for the Quick Analysis button, which you'll find in the lower-right section of the selected data.
- Alternatively, you can use the shortcut Ctrl + Q.
- Click on the Charts option.
- Hover over the different chart types to get a preview of how they would look with your data. Once you find the one you want, select it.

- If you want to explore more chart options, click on "More" and then "All Charts" to see the full range of choices. When you're satisfied, click OK to insert the chart into your document.

Chapter 4: Excel's Data Sorting

4.1 Sorting Data in a Worksheet

In a worksheet, you have the ability to organize and rearrange information to easily locate specific values. This can be done by sorting a range or table of data based on one or more columns. Let's say you want to sort employees. You can first sort them by department and then further refine the sorting by last name. By doing so, you can quickly find the desired information you're looking for.

4.2 How Can I Use Excel to Sort?

To sort your data using Excel, follow these steps:

4.2.1 Choosing Which Data to Sort

To work with tabular data in spreadsheets, you can choose a specific range of cells. This range can include multiple columns and rows, like A1:P8, or just a single column, like D1:D90. You can even add the first row that contains the headings for each column. This allows you to focus on the data you need and perform operations or analysis on that selected range.

4.2.2 Quick and Simple Sorting

- To sort a column in Excel, start by choosing a cell in that column.
- Then, go to the Data tab and locate the Sort & Filter group.
- Click on the command that arranges the data in ascending order (A to Z, or smallest to largest). This will organize the column from A to Z, or from the smallest number to the largest.
- Conversely, if you want to sort the column in descending order (from Z to A or largest to smallest), click on the corresponding command.

4.2.3 Sorting Using a Given Set of Criteria

Sorting your data by specifying criteria allows you to select the column you wish to sort while considering additional factors like cell colors or font styles.

- Begin by selecting a single cell within the range you wish to sort.
- Move to the Data tab and locate the Sort & Filter group. Click on the Sort option to open the popup window labeled "Sort."
- Choose the first column you wish to sort the data by in the Sort by drop-down menu.
- You have the option to select Values, Cell Icon, Font Color, or Cell Color in the Sort On list.
- Next, select the desired order from the order list. You can choose to sort numerically or alphabetically, either in descending or ascending order. For instance, you can sort numbers from higher to lower or lower to higher, or text from Z to A or A to Z.

4.3 How to Sort Multiple Columns

To sort data in multiple columns, follow these steps:

- Choose the data you want to sort or select a cell in the data set.
- Navigate to the Data tab and select the main sort button, not the smaller ones.

- A window will appear. If your data has headers and you've selected them, tick the box in the top right corner labeled "My data has headers." This ensures the headers won't be sorted along with the data.
- In Excel, we need to specify the sorting method. To do this, locate the Sort by section and click on the drop-down menu. From there, choose the first column you want to sort, which in our example is Column A.
- Next, find the Sort On drop-down menu and select the desired sorting criteria. For this particular case, we will keep them as values.
- Finally, navigate to the Order drop-down menu and select the preferred sorting order for the column.
- To continue, simply click on the "Add Level" button located at the top left corner of the window and follow the same process outlined in Steps 4–6.
- Repeat the previous steps (4–7) for each additional column you wish to sort. Keep in mind that the options in the "Order" drop-down menu may vary slightly depending on whether the column contains numbers or text, but they are fairly intuitive.
- Once you have finished configuring the sorting settings, click "OK," and you're all set! There's nothing more to it.

Key Points

- This technique is simple yet highly effective when working with extensive datasets that have multiple columns.
- Before applying this method to crucial data, it's advisable to practice on a smaller dataset to grasp the process. Avoid sorting a subset of data while leaving the rest unsorted.
- If a sorting error occurs, use Ctrl + Z to undo the action and start again.
- To modify the sorting order, select the desired row in the Sort window and use the arrow buttons on the left of the Options button (refer to Step 8 for a clear view). Sorting begins with the higher rows.

4.4 Custom Sort Order

Excel offers a convenient feature that allows you to arrange data in a specific order of your choosing. For instance, suppose you have a dataset and want to sort it based on priority levels such as high, normal, and low. In such cases, Excel provides a simple and effective solution.

- To begin sorting your data set, click on any cell within it.
- Next, navigate to the Data tab and locate the Sort & Filter group. Within this group, you will find the sort option. Selecting this will open the Sort dialog box.

- From the 'Sort by' drop-down list, choose Priority.
- Then, from the 'Order' drop-down list, select Custom List. This will bring up the Custom Lists dialog box.
- Here, you can enter the desired list entries.
- Afterward, click OK, and then OK again.

As a result, your records will be sorted based on their priority, with the options being High, Normal, and Low.

4.5 How to Sort a Row

To rearrange your data, you have the option to sort it by row instead of column. Let's say you have a table of monthly sales, and you want to arrange it in such a way that the month with the highest sales appears on the left. To achieve this, you can make use of a handy right-click popup menu.

To arrange data by a specific row, you can follow these steps:

- Begin by choosing a cell within the row you wish to sort.
- Press Ctrl + A to select the entire range of data.
- Verify that the selected area encompasses all the necessary data.
- Right-click on a cell within the desired row.
- From the menu that appears, select the option for sorting, followed by "Custom Sort."
- In the Sort dialog box, locate the "Sort By" box and choose the day column as the sorting criterion.
- Choose Custom List in the Order drop-down menu.
- In the Sort dialog box, click the Options button located at the top.
- Go to Orientation within the Sort Options dialog box and choose Sort Left to Right.
- Click OK to exit the Options dialog box.

- Now, select the specific row you wish to sort from the Sort By drop-down menu.
- Since there are no headings, choose the appropriate row number.
- Select the desired sort-on and order options.
- Finally, click OK to apply the sorting and have the data arranged according to the values in the selected row.

4.6 Sorting the Order of Conditional Formatting Rules

In situations where multiple rules are assigned to a specific range, it is possible for a single cell to meet the criteria of two or more rules. In such cases, it may become necessary to rearrange the order of the rules to ensure that the most significant formatting takes precedence. This ensures that the desired formatting is correctly applied to the cell.

To change the order of conditional formatting rules in Excel, follow these steps:

- Begin by selecting a cell within the range that contains multiple conditional formatting rules.
- On the Home tab, locate and click the Conditional Formatting button.

- From the drop-down menu, choose the option labeled "Manage Rules."
- In the dialog box that appears, you will find a list of the rules associated with the selected range.
- Locate and select the rule that you wish to reposition.
- To adjust its position, use the Move Up or Move Down arrow buttons.
- Once the rule is in the desired position, click OK.

By rearranging the rules in this manner, you can determine the order in which they are applied, ensuring that the rule at the top of the list takes precedence.

4.7 Filtering Data in Excel

To narrow down a range of data in Excel, follow these steps:

- Pick any cell within the desired range.
- Go to the Data tab and click on the Filter option.
- Click on the arrow next to the column header to open the filter menu.
- Choose either number filters or text filters, then select a comparison option like "Between."
- Enter the filter criteria and click OK to apply the filter.

Chapter 5: Working with Excel Charts and Tables

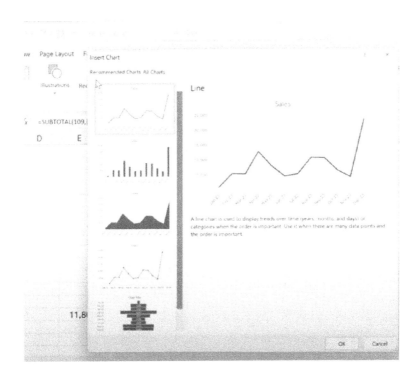

5.1 What Makes an Excel Table Necessary?

In Excel, tables serve as containers for organizing your data. By designating a range of rows and columns as a table, you indicate to Excel that these elements are interconnected. This has two major advantages. First, it provides you with numerous built-in features for managing lists. Secondly, whenever you insert a new row, the formulas and formatting are automatically applied. This saves you valuable time and ensures that your data remains consistent and organized.

5.2 How Can a Table Be Created in Excel?

Creating an Excel table in Microsoft Excel is a straightforward process. Here's how you can do it:

- Open your Excel workbook and choose the worksheet that contains your list.
- You can either manually select the range of cells that make up your list or let Excel automatically select them for you.
- Next, click on the "Insert" tab and choose "Table." That's it!

Once created, your list will transform into a table with a default blue design. The table will come with built-in filters and locked headers, making it easier to work with your data. It's a good practice to give your table a meaningful name instead of the default names like Table1, Table2, etc. This helps in quickly identifying and referring to specific tables.

5.3 Creating Pivot Charts and Tables

5.3.1 A Pivot Table: What Is It?

A pivot table is a valuable tool that helps you make sense of your data and identify trends. It allows you to analyze and compare different values in a clear and concise manner. Think of it as a way to organize and extract meaning from the overwhelming numbers on your screen.

The term "pivot" refers to the ability to rotate or reorganize the data in the table. This flexibility allows you to view your data from various angles and draw meaningful insights.

Creating a pivot table may seem intimidating at first, but don't be worried! With this step-by-step approach, you can quickly become proficient in using this powerful Excel feature. In this detailed guide, I will walk you through the process of creating a pivot table in just a few simple steps. Once you grasp the basics, you'll be able to confidently harness the power of pivot tables in Excel.

5.3.2 Using Excel to Make Pivot Tables

- To begin, you'll need to create a pivot table. Start by selecting the data you wish to analyze. You can do this by either clicking the triangle at the top left or pressing CTRL + A to select everything. Next, go to the top menu and click on Insert, then select Pivot Table.

- Once you have your pivot table, it's time to arrange the variables in the appropriate boxes. There are four boxes available: filters, columns, rows, and values. How you organize them will depend on the specific questions you want to answer.

- Now, let's set the calculation. In the "values" box, drag the variable you want to analyze and choose the calculation you wish to apply. The most commonly used calculations are SUM and AVERAGE.

- Finally, you can sort the data in descending order. Right-click on the table, select sort, and then choose sort from largest to smallest. This will arrange the data from highest to lowest.

5.3.3 Using Excel to Create Pivot Charts

At times, it can be challenging to grasp the overall concept when your unprocessed data is yet to be condensed. Your initial inclination might be to generate a pivot table. However, not everyone possesses the ability to interpret numerical data in a tabular format and immediately discern the underlying patterns. This is where pivot charts come into play, as they serve as an excellent tool to incorporate visual representations into your data analysis.

5.3.4 Putting Together a Pivot Chart

To make a pivot chart using Excel, you can follow these steps:

- Choose a cell within your table.
- Go to the Insert tab and click on PivotChart.
- Decide where you want the pivot chart to be placed.
- Click on OK.
- Select the fields you want to show in the menu.

5.3.5 Creating a Chart from a PivotTable

To generate a chart from a pivot table, here's what you can do:

- Choose any cell within your table.
- Go to PivotTable Tools, then click on Analyze, followed by PivotChart.
- Pick a chart that suits your needs.
- Click OK to confirm your selection.

5.4 A Deep Dive into Excel Charts

5.4.1 How Do You Define an Excel Chart?

A chart is a visual tool that displays data in rows and columns. It helps analyze patterns and trends in data sets. For example, if you've been tracking sales figures in Excel for three years, charts can quickly show you which year had the highest and lowest sales. You can also use charts to compare actual achievements with set targets. They simplify the interpretation of data and provide valuable insights.

5.4.2 Microsoft Excel Chart Types

In various situations, you may need different types of charts. Luckily, Excel offers a range of chart options to suit your needs. The choice of chart depends on the kind of data you wish to present visually. To make things easier for users, Excel 2013 and later versions come with a feature that analyzes your data and suggests the most suitable chart type for you to use. This way, you can effortlessly showcase your data in a visually appealing manner.

In the vast world of Excel charts, there are several popular options to choose from. Let's explore some of these charts and their ideal use cases.

5.4.2.1 Pie Chart

This chart is perfect for quantifying items and presenting them as percentages. It provides a clear visual representation of how each item contributes to the whole.

5.4.2.2 Bar Chart

If you're looking to compare values across a few categories, the bar chart is your go-to. It presents data with bars that run horizontally, allowing for easy comparison between categories.

5.4.2.3 Combo Chart

Sometimes, you may need to highlight different types of information simultaneously. In such cases, the combo chart comes in handy. It allows you to blend different chart types, providing a comprehensive view of the data.

5.4.2.4 Column Chart

Similar to the bar chart, the column chart is used to compare values across categories. However, in this case, the values are presented vertically, offering a different perspective on the data.

5.4.2.5 Line Chart

When it comes to visualizing trends over time, such as monthly, daily, or yearly data, the line chart is an excellent choice. It helps identify patterns and fluctuations in the data with its continuous line.

5.5 Inserting Excel Charts into Your Worksheet

Creating a chart in Excel is a straightforward process. In this example, we will plot a basic Excel column chart. Here's a step-by-step guide:

- Launch Excel on your computer.
- Choose the data that you wish to display on the chart.
- Locate the INSERT tab in the ribbon at the top.
- Look for the drop-down button labeled "Column Chart" and click on it.
- From the options presented, select the specific chart type that suits your needs. Your desired chart will now be visible.

5.6 Changing the Chart Type of an Existing Chart

You have the ability to modify the appearance of an existing chart by altering its style.

In the case of most 2-D charts, you can change the entire chart's type to give it a fresh appearance. Alternatively, you can select a different chart type for a specific data series, resulting in a combination chart. However, for bubble charts and all 3-D charts, you are limited to changing the chart type for the entire chart.

Please note that to execute this task, you must first possess a preexisting chart.

- To change your chart type in Excel, you have a couple of options. First, if you want to change the chart type for the entire chart, simply click on the plot area or chart area to access the chart tools. Alternatively, you can right-click on the plot area or chart area and select "Change Chart Type."
- If you wish to change the chart type for a specific data series, just click on that particular series. Keep in mind that you can only change the chart type for one data series at a time. If you want to modify

multiple data series, you'll need to repeat the process for each one.

- Once you've accessed the chart tools, you'll see the Design, Layout, and Format tabs. Click on the Design tab and locate the Type group. From there, click on "Change Chart Type."
- A dialog box will appear, displaying various chart types for you to choose from. The first box presents different chart type categories, while the second box shows the available chart types within each category.
- Lastly, if you have previously saved a chart template and would like to use it, click on the "Templates" option and select the desired template.

5.7 Changing the Style of Your Excel Chart

One convenient method for altering the appearance of a chart is to utilize the pre-existing layouts and styles found in Excel. These options provide a quick and effective means of modifying the visual presentation of your chart.

5.7.1 Applying a Chart Layout

In-built chart layouts enable swift modifications to a chart's general arrangement by employing various arrangements of chart orientations, labels, and titles.

- First, choose the chart you wish to format.
- Then, navigate to the Design tab.
- Look for the Quick Layout button and click on it.
- Finally, pick the layout that best suits your needs. This layout will be applied to your chart.

5.7.2 Applying a Chart Style

With the help of built-in chart styles, you have the power to modify the appearance of multiple chart elements simultaneously. These styles make it effortless to alter shading, colors, and other formatting attributes in a jiffy.

- Choose the chart you want to modify.
- Access the Design tab.
- Locate the Chart Styles More button. If the desired style is already visible in the gallery, you can simply select it without expanding the menu.
- Opt for a different style that suits your needs.

5.7.3 Changing Colors

To customize the appearance of a style without altering its overall design, you can simply modify the colors to align with your preferences. Here's how you can do it:

- Choose the chart you want to modify.

- Navigate to the Design tab.
- Locate and click on the Change Colors button.
- From the options presented, select a different color set.
- The chart will be updated with the new color scheme you've chosen.

5.8 Switching Columns and Rows in a Chart

In Excel, you have the option to switch the column and row orientation of data in a chart. By default, Excel suggests using columns for the vertical axis and rows for the horizontal axis in charts. However, if you want to change this arrangement, you can easily switch the column and row positions. This action effectively swaps the vertical and horizontal axes in your chart, giving you more flexibility in presenting your data.

- Choose the chart you wish to modify.
- Go to the Chart Design tab on the Excel ribbon.
- Look for the button that says "Switch Row/Column.".
- Click on this button.
- Your chart will now have a different orientation, with the rows representing the vertical axis and the columns representing the horizontal axis.

For those who find convenience in keyboard shortcuts, here are a few you can utilize:

- To choose the specific chart you wish to modify, simply select it.
- If you'd like to create a chart swiftly, press Alt + F1.
- To toggle between switching the row and column, press F11.

5.9 How to Resize a Chart

In case the chart appears too small or too large, you have the option to adjust its size.

- Simply navigate to Chart Tools and select the Format tab.
- From there, locate the Size group and make the necessary resizing adjustments to ensure the chart fits appropriately.

Chapter 6: Mathematical Functions in Excel

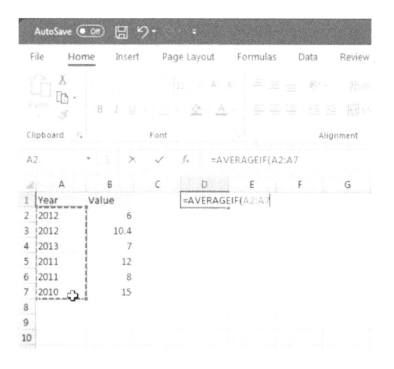

Mathematical functions in Excel are built-in formulas that perform calculations on numeric data. They are designed to simplify complex calculations and help users analyze and manipulate data efficiently. Excel offers a wide range of mathematical functions, including basic arithmetic operations like addition, subtraction, multiplication, and division. It also provides more advanced functions, such as trigonometric functions, statistical functions, and financial functions. These functions can be used to perform calculations on individual cells, ranges of cells, or entire columns of data.

Now, let's delve into each of these functions and explore them thoroughly.

6.1 The SUM Function

The SUM function in Excel is a powerful tool that allows you to add up a range of numbers quickly and efficiently. It simplifies the process of totaling values in a spreadsheet, making calculations very easy.

To use the SUM function, you need to follow a specific syntax. Here's how it works:

=SUM(number1, number2,...)

In this syntax, "number1" and "number2" represent the values you want to add together. You can include as many numbers as you need, separating them with commas. It's important to note that you can also use cell references instead of actual numbers.

Let's take a simple example to illustrate how the SUM function works. Imagine you have a spreadsheet with three values in cells A1, A2, and A3: 5, 10, and 15, respectively. To find the sum of these numbers, you would use the following formula:

=SUM(A1, A2, A3)

When you press enter, Excel will calculate the sum and display the result in the cell where you entered the formula. In this case, the sum would be 30.

6.2 The AVERAGE Function

The AVERAGE function in Excel is a useful tool that calculates the average of a range of numbers. Its syntax is straightforward: "=AVERAGE(number1, number2,...)" or "=AVERAGE(range)".

For example, let's say we have a range of numbers: 5, 10, 15, 20. To find the average, we can use the formula "=AVERAGE(5, 10, 15, 20)" or "=AVERAGE(A1:A4)" if the numbers are in cells A1 to A4. The result will be 12.5, which is the sum of the numbers (50) divided by the count (4).

By using the AVERAGE function, you can easily calculate the average of any given set of numbers in Excel.

6.3 The AVERAGEIF Function

The AVERAGEIF function in Excel allows you to calculate the average of a range of cells based on a specific condition. It is a useful tool for analyzing data and extracting meaningful insights. The syntax of the AVERAGEIF function is straightforward: =AVERAGEIF(range, criteria, [average_range]).

. "range" refers to the range of cells that you want to evaluate.

. "criteria" specifies the condition that needs to be met, and "average_range" (optional) defines the range of cells that you want to average.

Here's a simple example to demonstrate how the AVERAGEIF function works. Let's say you have a dataset of students' test scores in column A, and you want to find the average score of all the students who scored above 80. You can use the AVERAGEIF function as follows:

=AVERAGEIF(A1:A10, ">80")

In this example, A1:A10 is the range of cells containing the test scores, and ">80" is the criteria that specifies the condition for the scores to be above 80. Excel will calculate the average of all the scores that meet this condition and display the result.

6.4 The COUNTA function

The COUNTA function in Excel is a tool that allows you to count the number of cells in a range that contain any type of data, including text, numbers, and even empty cells. It is commonly used to determine the total number of entries in a given range.

Syntax: COUNTA(value1, [value2],...)

Example: Let's say you have a range of cells (A1:A5) containing the following data: "Apple," 25, "", "Orange," and "Banana." By using the COUNTA function as follows: =COUNTA(A1:A5), you would get a result of 4. This is because there are four cells in the range that contain data, excluding the empty cell.

6.5 The COUNTIF function

The COUNTIF function in Excel is a powerful tool that allows you to count the number of cells in a range that meet a specific criterion. It comes in handy when you want to analyze data and get a quick count of how many times a certain condition is met.

The syntax for the COUNTIF function is straightforward. It consists of two arguments: the range and the criteria. The range represents the cells you want to search for, and the criteria define the condition you want to check for.

Here's a simple example to illustrate how the COUNTIF function works. Let's say you have a column of numbers in cells A1 to A10, and you want to count how many of those numbers are greater than 5.

To do that, you would use the formula =COUNTIF(A1:A10,">5"). This formula tells Excel to count the number of cells in the range A1 to A10 that are greater than 5. The result will be the count of cells that meet this condition.

6.6 The ROUND function

The ROUND function in Excel is a handy tool that allows you to round a number to a specified number of decimal places. Its syntax is quite straightforward: =ROUND(number, num_digits).

Let's break it down. The "number" argument represents the value you want to round. It can be a cell reference or a numerical value. The "num_digits" argument indicates the number of decimal places to which you want to round the number.

To illustrate, suppose you have the number 3.14159 in cell A1. If you want to round it to two decimal places, you can use the formula =ROUND(A1, 2). Excel will then round the number to 3.14.

6.7 Key Points to Keep in Mind

- The mathematical functions in Excel are grouped together in the "Math & Trigonometry" function category.
- When a cell reference is used in a formula, the formula will adjust dynamically. Any changes made to the referenced cells will be immediately reflected in the formula cells.

- The COUNTA function counts all non-empty cells, while the COUNT function in Excel only calculates numeric cell values.

Chapter 7: Financial Functions in Excel

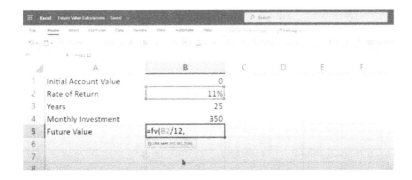

7.1 Excel's Financial Functions: What Are They?

Excel provides a range of predefined formulas known as financial functions, which are designed to perform various calculations related to finance. These functions are valuable tools for finance professionals as they allow for the analysis of financial data, investment decision-making, interest rate calculations, payment scheduling, and risk and return evaluation. With a wide array of financial functions available, Excel offers a comprehensive solution for addressing different financial scenarios.

7.2 The FV (Future Value) Function

The future value (FV) is a useful metric for assessing the worth of an investment or a series of payments. It takes into account the interest rate and the number of periods involved. To calculate the FV, you can use the following formula:

FV(rate, nper, pmt, [pv], [type])

Here's what each parameter represents:

- Rate: This refers to the interest rate per period for the investment. It represents the rate at which the investment grows or accumulates value.
- Nper: This represents the total number of payment periods or the duration of the investment. It helps determine how long the investment will last.
- Pmt: This indicates the payment made at each period. It represents the regular contributions made towards the investment.
- [pv]: This is an optional argument that represents the present value or the initial investment amount. If provided, it signifies the value of the investment at the start, before considering any payments or interest. If omitted, assume it is zero.
- [type]: This is also an optional argument that specifies the timing of the payments within each period. If omitted, assume it is 0, indicating that payments are made at the end of each period. If set to 1, payments are made at the beginning of each period.

7.3 The PV (Present Value) Function

The PV function is a useful tool for determining the present value of an investment or a series of cash flows. This calculation takes into account the time period and the discount rate involved. The syntax of the PV function is quite straightforward: PV(rate, nper, pmt, [fv], [type])

To use the PV function, you'll need to input the following parameters:

- First, we have the rate, which represents the interest rate per period.
- Then, we have the Nper, which refers to the total number of payment periods or cash flows. This helps determine the investment's duration or the number of periods in which the cash flows occur.
- Next, we have the Pmt, which represents the cash flow amount or payment that takes place in each period. This can be a fixed value or an annuity, which refers to a series of equal payments.
- Additionally, we have the [Fv] option, which is not mandatory. It denotes the desired future value or cash balance at the end of the last period. If this value is not provided, Excel assumes it to be zero.
- Lastly, we have the [Type] option, which is also not mandatory. It specifies whether the payment occurs

at the beginning (type = 1) or end (type = 0) of each period. If this option is omitted, Excel assumes it to be 0, representing the end of the period.

7.4 The IRR (Internal Rate of Return) Function

The Internal Rate of Return (IRR) is a metric used to determine the rate at which the present value of cash inflows and outflows is equal. To calculate the IRR, you can use the formula IRR(values, [guess]).

- Values: This required input represents the range of cash flows or values for the purposes for which you intend to determine the internal rate of return. These cash flows may be positive or negative, and they need to have no fewer than one negative and one positive cash flow. A sequence of cash flows over time must be represented by the values in chronological order.
- [guess]: Your estimate or guess of the internal rate of return is reflected by this optional input. Excel will make a default approximation of 0.1 (10%) if you leave this argument out. Especially in situations where there are many possible rates of return, giving a guess can be helpful in the function's faster convergence.
- Let's say we have an investment plan that spans three years and has cash inflows of $2,000, $3,000,

and $5,000. To calculate the internal rate of return, we can use the formula =IRR(-2000, 3000, 5000).

7.5 The NPV (Net Present Value) Function

The net present value (NPV) is a measure used to determine the value of an investment. It calculates this value by discounting the cash inflows and outflows at a specified rate.

To calculate NPV, you need to consider two main factors:

- Rate: This refers to the discount rate or the required rate of return for the investment. It represents the interest rate used to discount future cash flows back to their present value. For example, if you use a rate of 10%, it means each future cash flow will be discounted by 10% per period.
- Value1, value2, etc.: These values represent the cash flows occurring at different periods. They can be positive or negative. Value1 indicates the cash flow at period 1, while Value2 and so on represent the cash flows at subsequent periods. It's important to input the cash flows on a regular basis and in sequential order (e.g., quarterly, monthly, or annually) for the NPV function to work correctly.

Here's an example to help illustrate the calculation:

Suppose you have an investment that will receive $2,000, $5,000, and $3,000 over the duration of 3 years, and you want to apply a 10% discount rate. You can use the following formula to calculate the project's net present value: =NPV(0.10, 2000, 5000, 3000).

7.6 The RATE Function

Determining the interest rate for an investment or loan can be done using the RATE function. This function takes into account the payment amount and the number of periods to calculate the interest rate per period.

The formula for the RATE function is as follows: RATE(nper, pmt, pv, [fv], [type], [guess])

- Nper refers to the overall number of payment periods. It basically tells you how long the loan or investment will last.
- The payment for each period, known as the PMT, remains consistent throughout the duration of the loan or investment. This payment encompasses both the interest and principal components, ensuring a steady repayment structure.

- In financial terms, the present value (PV) refers to the initial loan or investment amount. It represents the current sum of money that you possess or the amount that has been borrowed.
- The future value [fv] is an optional parameter. It signifies the anticipated or desired value of an investment at the conclusion of the investment period. If this parameter is not specified, it is assumed to be zero.
- The [type] parameter (optional) determines if the payments are made at the start or end of the period. When not specified, it is assumed to be zero, indicating payments made at the end of the period.
- [guess]: This argument is optional. It refers to a guess or estimate of the interest rate. It serves as the beginning area for the calculations in Excel. Excel considers it to be 0.05 (5%) if it is left empty.

7.7 The PMT (Payment) Function

The PMT function helps you determine the regular payment needed to pay off a loan or investment. It takes into account factors like the interest rate, the number of payment periods, and the initial amount borrowed or invested.

The formula for PMT is as follows: PMT(rate, nper, pv, [fv], [type])

- Rate: This denotes the rate of interest for an investment or loan, expressed per period. If required, it should be divided by the number of periods in a year.
- Nper refers to the overall number of payment periods for the investment or loan. This figure is typically expressed in months or years; this depends on how often payments are made.
- The present value, often abbreviated as Pv, refers to the initial investment or principal amount. It signifies the total sum invested or borrowed at the start.
- The optional argument [Fv] denotes the desired balance or future value after you make the final payment. If not specified, it is assumed to be zero.
- The [Type] argument is not mandatory. It specifies whether the payment is due at the beginning (type=1) or end (type=0) of each period. If you don't specify the type, the default assumption is that the payment is due at the end of the month and is therefore zero.
- Consider this illustration: Let's say you have borrowed $50,000 with an interest rate of 5% and a loan duration of 10 years. To calculate the monthly payment, you can use a formula like this: =PMT(0.0512, 1012, 50000).

7.8 The MAX and MIN Function

The MAX and MIN functions are used to find the highest and lowest values within a specified set of numbers. To use the MAX function, you simply input the numbers you want to compare, separated by commas. The function will return the largest number from the provided set. Similarly, the MIN function works in the same way but returns the smallest number instead.

The formulas for the MAX and MIN functions are as follows: MAX(number1, [number2],...) and MIN(number1, [number2],...)

- The initial cell reference or number you would like to compare is referred to as [Number1].
- [number2]: This argument is optional. To compare with the initial number, you can add more cell references or numbers that are separated by commas. The total amount of "number" arguments you can have is 255.

For instance, let's say you have a range of values in cells A1 to A12, and you would like to find the maximum value in that range. In this case, you can use the formula =MAX(A1:A12) to determine the highest value.

7.9 A Few Tips for Making the Most of Financial Functions

- It is crucial to have a solid grasp of the syntax of every financial function in Excel. This means understanding the specific format and order in which the inputs should be provided.

- Take advantage of the help resources available in Excel. These resources offer comprehensive documentation and examples for every financial function. By consulting these resources, you can gain a clear understanding of the purpose and usage of each function.

- Instead of directly entering values into a function, consider using cell references. This makes it possible to update and modify data with simplicity without needing to change the financial formulas in your spreadsheet.

- Excel provides the capability to carry out intricate calculations and enables the combined use of several financial functions. Take advantage of this feature to automate monotonous operations and develop sophisticated financial models.

- Conduct Sensitivity Analysis. Modify the input parameters to see how they affect the result. Sensitivity analysis facilitates improved decision-making by determining how sensitive financial models are to different inputs.

Chapter 8: Logical Functions in Excel

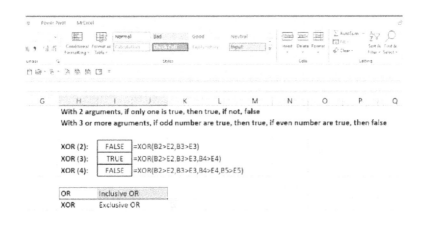

Microsoft Excel offers a set of logical functions that allow users to work with logical values. These functions come in handy when you need to perform multiple comparisons in a formula or test multiple conditions simultaneously. Along with logical operators, these functions evaluate the arguments and return either true or false. This feature allows users to create complex formulas and make decisions based on logical outcomes.

8.1 The AND Function

The AND function in Excel is a logical function that allows you to check if all the conditions specified are true. It returns TRUE if all the conditions are met and FALSE if any of the conditions are not met.

The syntax for the AND function is:

=AND(logical1, [logical2],...)

Where logical1, logical2, and so on are the conditions you want to check. You can have up to 255 conditions.

To explain the syntax, the AND function takes one or more logical expressions as arguments. These logical expressions are separated by commas.

Here's a simple example to illustrate the use of the AND function:

=AND(A1>10, B1<20)

In this example, the AND function checks if the value in cell A1 is greater than 10 and the value in cell B1 is less than 20. If both conditions are true, the AND function will return true. Otherwise, it will return false.

Using the AND function can be helpful in scenarios where you need to analyze data and make decisions based on multiple conditions being met simultaneously.

8.2 The OR Function

The OR function in Excel is a logical function that allows you to check multiple conditions and return a true or false value based on the result. Its syntax is straightforward and easy to understand.

Syntax: =OR(condition1, condition2,...)

Explanation: The OR function takes one or more conditions as arguments and evaluates them. It returns TRUE if at least one of the conditions is TRUE, and FALSE if all the conditions are FALSE.

Example: Let's say we have a dataset of students and their exam scores in columns A and B. To determine if a student passed the exam (scored 70 or above), we can use the OR function. In cell C2, we would enter the following formula:

=OR(A2>=70, B2>=70)

This formula checks if either the score in column A or column B is equal to or greater than 70. If either of the conditions is true, the formula returns TRUE; otherwise, it returns FALSE.

8.3 The XOR Function

The XOR function in Excel is a logical function that returns TRUE if one and only one of the given conditions is TRUE. It stands for "exclusive OR." The syntax for the XOR function is:

=XOR(logical1, logical2,...)

The logical1, logical2, etc. are the conditions or expressions that you want to evaluate. You can have up to 255 conditions within the XOR function. Each logical argument should be separated by a comma.

Here's a simple example to illustrate how the XOR function works. Let's say we have two cells: A1 and B1. In A1, we have the value TRUE, and in B1, we have the value false. We can use the XOR function in another cell, C1, to determine if only one of these conditions is true. The formula would be:

=XOR(A1, B1)

In this case, the XOR function would return TRUE because only one of the conditions is true.

8.4 The NOT Function

The NOT function in Excel is a logical function that reverses the logical value of a given expression or condition. It returns the opposite of the logical value. The syntax for the NOT function is straightforward: =NOT(logical). Here, "logical" can be any expression or condition that evaluates to either true or false.

To better understand the syntax, let's consider a simple example. Suppose we have a column of values in cells A1 to A5, and we want to check if any of these values are less than 10. We can use the NOT function to reverse the logical value. In cell B1, we can write the formula =NOT(A1<10). This formula will return TRUE if the value in cell A1 is not less than 10 and FALSE if it is less than 10. We can then copy this formula down to cells B2 to B5 to check the remaining values.

8.5 The IF Function

The IF function in Excel is a powerful tool that allows you to perform conditional calculations based on specific criteria. With this function, you can instruct Excel to execute different actions depending on whether a certain condition is met or not.

The syntax of the IF function consists of three main components: the logical test, the value_if_true, and the value_if_false. The logical test is the condition that you want Excel to evaluate. The value_if_true is the result or action that should be taken if the condition is true, while the value_if_false is the result or action that should be taken if the condition is false.

To better understand the syntax, let's consider a simple example. Imagine you have a list of students and their corresponding grades in columns A and B, respectively. You want to assign a pass or fail status to each student based on their grade. In this case, you can use the IF function to accomplish this task.

In cell C2, you can enter the following formula:

=IF(B2>=60,"Pass","Fail")

In this formula, the logical test is B2>=60, which checks if the grade in cell B2 is greater than or equal to 60. If it is, the value_if_true is "Pass," indicating that the student has passed. If the condition is false, the value_if_false is "Fail," indicating that the student has failed.

By dragging the formula down to apply it to the remaining cells in column C, Excel will automatically evaluate each student's grade and assign the pass or fail status accordingly.

The IF function in Excel is a versatile tool that can be used in various scenarios, such as financial analysis, data validation, and decision-making processes. Understanding its syntax and how to apply it effectively will greatly enhance your ability to work with data in Excel.

8.6 The IFERROR Function

The IFERROR function in Excel is a powerful tool that allows you to handle errors in formulas. It helps streamline your spreadsheet by providing a way to handle errors without causing your entire formula to fail. The syntax of the IFERROR function is straightforward:

IFERROR(value, value_if_error)

The first argument, value, is the expression or formula you want to evaluate. The second argument, value_if_error, is the value or action you want Excel to perform if the first argument returns an error.

For example, let's say you have a formula that divides two numbers:

=A1/B1

If B1 is 0, this formula will result in a #DIV/0! error. To handle this error gracefully, you can use the IFERROR function like this:

=IFERROR(A1/B1, 0)

In this case, if B1 is 0, the IFERROR function will return 0 instead of the error. This helps prevent your entire spreadsheet from being filled with error messages and allows you to continue working with accurate data.

Chapter 9: Statistical Functions in Excel

D2		×	✓	fx	=VAR.S(A2:A16)

	A	B	C	D	E
1	Fish X length (cm)				
2	81		Variance	=VAR.S(A2:A16)	
3	71		St. dev.		
4	52				
5	100				
6	104				

Here are some commonly used statistical functions that can be quite useful: They include the COUNT, COUNTA, COUNTBLANK, and COUNTIFS functions. Let's take a closer look at each one:

9.1 The COUNT Function

The COUNT function in Excel is a powerful tool that allows you to determine the number of cells within a range that contain numerical values. It can be particularly useful when you're working with large datasets and need to quickly assess how many values are present.

The syntax of the COUNT function is straightforward. It takes one argument, which is the range of cells you want to count. You simply need to enclose the range in parentheses after the COUNT keyword.

For example, let's say you have a column of numbers in cells A1 to A10, and you want to count how many cells in that range contain values. To do this, you would use the following formula:

=COUNT(A1:A10)

This formula will return the count of cells in the range of A1 to A10 that contain numerical values. It's important to note that the COUNT function only counts cells that contain numbers; it ignores empty cells or cells that contain text or errors.

9.2 The COUNTA Function

The COUNTA function in Excel is a useful tool for counting the number of cells in a range that contain any type of data, including text, numbers, and logical values. It allows you to quickly determine the total count of non-empty cells in a selected range.

The syntax for the COUNTA function is as follows:

=COUNTA(value1, [value2],...)

The "value1, value2,..." part represents the range or multiple ranges of cells that you want to count. You can specify up to 255 different ranges or individual cells as arguments.

For example, let's say you have a range of cells from A1 to A5, and you want to count how many of these cells contain data. You would use the COUNTA formula as follows:

=COUNTA(A1:A5)

This will return the total count of non-empty cells in the specified range.

The COUNTA function is particularly useful when you need to analyze data sets with missing or incomplete information. It allows you to quickly identify the number of cells that contain data, which can be crucial for statistical analysis, data validation, or simply keeping track of your data.

9.3 The COUNTBLANK Function

The COUNTBLANK function in Excel is a powerful tool that allows you to count the number of empty cells within a selected range. It comes in handy when you want to quickly determine the number of blank cells in a dataset without manually scanning through each cell.

To use the COUNTBLANK function, you need to follow a specific syntax. The syntax is as follows:

=COUNTBLANK(range)

The "range" parameter refers to the range of cells that you want to evaluate for blank cells. It can be a single cell or a range of cells.

Here's a simple example to illustrate how the COUNTBLANK function works. Let's say we have a column of data in cells A1 to A5, and we want to find out how many cells in that range are blank.

To do this, we would enter the following formula in an empty cell:

=COUNTBLANK(A1:A5)

After pressing Enter, Excel will return the count of blank cells in the specified range.

9.4 The COUNTIFS Function

The COUNTIFS function in Excel allows you to count the number of cells in a range that meet multiple criteria. It comes in handy when you need to analyze data that satisfies specific conditions. The syntax for the COUNTIFS function is as follows:

=COUNTIFS(range1, criteria1, range2, criteria2,...)

Let's break down the syntax:

- range1, range2,... These are the ranges or arrays you want to evaluate for the specified criteria.
- criteria1, criteria2,...: These are the conditions that the corresponding ranges must meet to be counted.

To better understand how it works, let's consider a simple example. Suppose you have a spreadsheet containing student grades for different subjects. You want to count how many students scored above 90 in math and above 80 in English. Here's how you can use the COUNTIFS function:

=COUNTIFS(Math_Grades, ">90", English_Grades, ">80")

In this example, Math_Grades and English_Grades represent the ranges containing the respective subject grades. The criteria ">90" and ">80" specify that the grades should be greater than 90 and 80, respectively. The COUNTIFS function will then count the number of cells that meet both conditions.

9.5 The MODE Function

The MODE function in Excel is a useful tool for finding the most frequently occurring value in a range of cells. Its syntax is straightforward and easy to understand. To use the MODE function, simply type "=MODE(" and then select the range of cells you want to analyze. The function will return the value that appears most frequently in the selected range.

For example, let's say we have a list of numbers in cells A1 to A10: 2, 4, 6, 4, 8, 2, 4, 10, 4, 6. If we use the MODE function by typing "=MODE(A1:A10)", Excel will return the value 4, as it appears most frequently in the range.

The MODE function is particularly useful when working with large datasets or when analyzing survey results. It allows you to quickly identify the most common value without having to manually scan through the data.

9.6 The STANDARD DEVIATION Function

The STANDARD DEVIATION function in Excel is a statistical function that calculates the standard deviation of a range of values. It measures the dispersion or variability of a dataset.

The syntax of the STANDARD DEVIATION function is "=STDEV(number1, [number2],...)", where "number1" is required and represents the values in the dataset. Additional numbers, up to a maximum of 255, can be included to calculate the standard deviation of multiple datasets.

The function returns the standard deviation as a numeric value. For example, if you have a dataset of test scores in cells A1 to A10, you can use the formula "=STDEV(A1:A10)" to calculate the standard deviation of the scores.

9.7 The VARIANCE Function

The VARIANCE function in Excel is a built-in statistical function that calculates the variance of a set of values. Its syntax is straightforward: =VAR(number1, [number2],...). The "number1" argument is required, while the "[number2],..." arguments are optional and represent additional numbers or ranges.

To explain the syntax further, the VARIANCE function takes the values you want to evaluate for variance. It can be a single value or a range of values. The function calculates the variance by measuring the dispersion or spread of the data points from their mean (average) value.

Here's a simple example to illustrate the usage of the VARIANCE function. Let's say we have a set of numbers in cells A1 to A5: 2, 4, 6, 8, and 10. To find the variance of these numbers, we would use the formula =VAR(A1:A5).

Excel will then calculate the variance and display the result in the cell where you entered the formula. The result would be 8, indicating the variance of the dataset.

The variance function is a powerful tool for analyzing data in Excel. It helps you understand how much individual data points deviate from the average, giving you insights into the variability of your data set. Whether you're analyzing financial data, evaluating test scores, or assessing the performance of a marketing campaign, the variance function can provide valuable information to aid in your decision-making process.

9.8 The QUARTILES Function

The QUARTILES function in Excel is a powerful tool that allows users to analyze data by dividing it into four equal parts, or quartiles. This function is commonly used in statistics and data analysis to understand the distribution of data points.

The syntax for the QUARTILES function is as follows: =QUARTILES(array, quart).

The "array" parameter represents the range of data you want to analyze, and the "quart" parameter specifies which quartile you want to calculate.

For example, let's say you have a dataset of student test scores in cells A1 to A10. To find the first quartile, you would use the formula =QUARTILES(A1:A10, 1). This will return the value that divides the data into the first 25% of the range.

9.9 The CORRELATION Function

Understanding the correlation function in Excel can greatly enhance your data analysis capabilities. This function allows you to determine the correlation coefficient between two sets of data, indicating the strength and direction of their relationship. To make the most of this powerful tool, it's important to grasp its syntax and how it works.

The syntax for the correlation function is straightforward. It takes two arguments, which are the two sets of data you want to analyze. For example, if you have a series of sales figures in column A and corresponding advertising expenses in column B, you can use the correlation function to assess the relationship between these two variables.

To use the correlation function, simply enter "=CORRELATION(range1, range2)" into a cell, replacing "range1" with the first set of data and "range2" with the second set. It's essential to ensure that both ranges contain the same number of data points.

For instance, let's say you want to determine the correlation between monthly sales and advertising expenses for a particular product. You have the sales figures in cells A2 to A13 and the corresponding advertising expenses in cells B2 to B13. In an empty cell, enter "=CORRELATION(A2:A13, B2:B13)" to calculate the correlation coefficient.

Once you press Enter, Excel will return a value between -1 and 1, indicating the strength and direction of the correlation. A value close to 1 signifies a strong positive correlation, meaning that as one variable increases, the other tends to increase as well. On the other hand, a value close to -1 suggests a strong negative correlation, implying that as one variable increases, the other tends to decrease. A value close to 0 indicates a weak or no correlation between the two variables.

Chapter 10: Text, Lookup, and Reference Functions in Excel

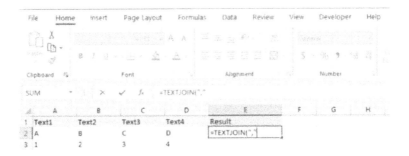

Lookup and reference functions in Excel are incredibly useful for searching for and retrieving specific data within a spreadsheet. In this chapter, we'll delve into the fundamentals of these functions and explore how they can enhance your spreadsheet proficiency.

In essence, Excel's lookup functions are designed to locate particular data within a defined range of cells and provide a corresponding value based on specified criteria. The most frequently used lookup functions include MATCH, INDEX, HLOOKUP, and VLOOKUP. These functions empower users to efficiently access and utilize data, streamlining the process of data retrieval and analysis.

10.1 The VLOOKUP Function

The VLOOKUP function in Excel allows users to find specific information within a large dataset. It stands for "Vertical Lookup" and is commonly used for tasks such as searching for a specific value in a table and retrieving related information from that table.

To understand the syntax of the VLOOKUP function, let's break it down:

=VLOOKUP(lookup_value, table_array, col_index_num, [range_lookup])

- lookup_value: This is the value you want to find in the leftmost column of the table. It can be a specific value or a cell reference.
- table_array: This is the range of cells that contain the data you want to search for. It should include at least two columns—the leftmost column should contain the lookup values, and the right column(s) should contain the related information you want to retrieve.
- col_index_num: This is the column number in the table_array from which you want to retrieve the data. The leftmost column is considered column number 1.

- range_lookup: This is an optional argument that determines whether you want an approximate match or an exact match. If you omit this argument, Excel assumes an approximate match, which can be useful for finding an approximate value in a sorted table.

Let's look at a simple example to illustrate how the VLOOKUP function works:

Suppose we have a table that contains the names of employees in column A and their corresponding salaries in column B. We want to find the salary of an employee named "Peter."

In an empty cell, we can enter the following formula:

=VLOOKUP("Peter", A1:B14, 2, FALSE)

Here's a breakdown of the formula:

- "Peter" is the lookup value we want to find.
- A1:B14 is the range of cells that contains our table data.

- 2 represents the second column in the table, which contains the salaries.
- FALSE is used to indicate that we want an exact match.

When we press Enter, Excel will search for "Peter" in the leftmost column of the table (column A). Once it finds a match, it will return the corresponding value from the second column (column B), which is the salary of "John."

10.2 The HLOOKUP Function

The HLOOKUP function in Excel allows you to search for a value in the top row of a table and return a corresponding value from a specified row. The syntax for the HLOOKUP function is as follows: =HLOOKUP(lookup_value, table_array, row_index_num, range_lookup).

Here's an example to illustrate its usage: Suppose you have a table with product names in the first row and corresponding prices in the second row. To find the price of a specific product, you can use the HLOOKUP function.

For instance, if you want to find the price of "Oranges," the formula would be =HLOOKUP("Oranges", A1:D2, 2,

FALSE). This will return the price of "Oranges" from the second row of the table.

10.3 The TRANSPOSE Function

The TRANSPOSE function in Excel is a powerful tool that allows you to flip the orientation of a range of cells. This function is particularly useful when you need to convert rows into columns or vice versa.

The syntax for the TRANSPOSE function is straightforward. Simply enter "=TRANSPOSE(range)" into a cell, where "range" refers to the range of cells you want to transpose.

To understand the syntax better, let's consider a simple example. Assume you have a row of data in cells A1 to G1, and you want to convert it into a column. In cell A2, you would enter "=TRANSPOSE(A1:G1)" and press Enter. Excel will then transpose the data, placing it vertically in cells A2 to A8.

10.4 The TRIM Function

The TRIM function in Excel is a useful tool that helps remove extra spaces from text. It is especially handy when dealing with data imported from other sources, where extra spaces can cause issues. The syntax of the TRIM function is straightforward: =TRIM(text). The "text" argument refers to the cell or range of cells from which you want to remove extra spaces.

For example, let's say you have a cell with the text " Hello, world! ". By using the TRIM function, you can eliminate the extra spaces and obtain "Hello, world!".

To apply the TRIM function, select the cell where you want the clean text to appear, enter the formula =TRIM(A1) (assuming the text is in cell A1), and press Enter. The trimmed text will now be displayed without the extra spaces. It's a simple yet effective way to clean up your data and ensure accuracy in your Excel spreadsheets.

10.5 The TEXTJOIN Function

The TEXTJOIN function in Excel allows you to combine multiple text strings into a single string. Its syntax is straightforward and easy to understand.

The syntax for the TEXTJOIN function is as follows:

=TEXTJOIN(delimiter, ignore_empty, text1, [text2],...)

Let's break down the syntax:

- Delimiter: This is the character or string that you want to use to separate the text strings. It can be a comma, a space, a hyphen, or any other character of your choice. Enclose the delimiter in double quotation marks if it's a string.
- Ignore_empty: This is an optional argument that determines whether empty cells should be ignored or included in the result. Use TRUE to ignore empty cells and FALSE to include them.
- Text1, [text2],... These are the text strings that you want to join together. You can include up to 253 text strings as arguments.

Now, let's look at a simple example to illustrate how the TEXTJOIN function works:

Suppose you have a list of names in cells A1:A5, and you want to join them together with a comma as the delimiter. You can use the following formula:

=TEXTJOIN(",", TRUE, A1:A5)

This formula will concatenate the names in cells A1 to A5, separating them with a comma. The result will be a single string with all the names joined together.

10.6 The PROPER Function

The PROPER function in Excel is a useful tool that helps you capitalize the first letter of each word in a text string. This function is particularly handy when you have a list of names or titles that need to be formatted correctly.

The syntax for the PROPER function is straightforward. Simply type "=PROPER(text)" into a cell, where "text" is the text string you want to modify. The function will then capitalize the first letter of each word in the text string.

For example, let's say you have a list of names in column A, starting from cell A1. To apply the PROPER function and capitalize the first letter of each name, you would enter "=PROPER(A1)" into cell B1. Then, you can simply drag the formula down to apply it to the rest of the names in column B.

10.7 The LOWER Function

The LOWER function in Excel is a simple yet robust tool that can transform text into lowercase letters. Its syntax is straightforward: =LOWER(text).

To break it down, "text" refers to the cell or text string that you want to convert to lowercase. You can either directly enter the text or reference a cell containing the text.

Let's say you have the word "HELLO" in cell A1. To convert it to lowercase using the LOWER function, you would enter the formula =LOWER(A1) in another cell. The result will be "hello" in all lowercase letters.

The lower function is handy when you need to standardize text or perform case-insensitive comparisons. It's a quick and efficient way to manipulate text data in Excel, making your tasks easier and more efficient.

Chapter 11: Improving Excel's Usability

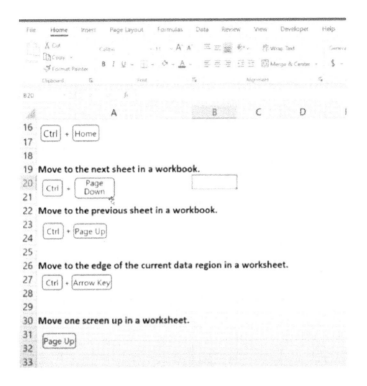

11.1 Excel Shortcuts

Please keep in mind that this list is not exhaustive, but it does contain some of the most useful Excel shortcuts. I hope you find them valuable and worth your while.

1. Ctrl + N

Create a new workbook and embark on a fresh Excel adventure.

2. Ctrl + O

Open an existing workbook and dive into your data.

3. Ctrl + S

Save your work and keep those precious formulas safe.

4. Ctrl + Z

Undo your last action and magically erase your mistakes.

5. Ctrl + Y

Redo what you just undid because we all make mistakes.

6. Ctrl + C

Copy a selected cell or range to the clipboard.

7. Ctrl + X

Cut a selected cell or range and prepare for a grand paste.

8. Ctrl + V

Paste the contents of the clipboard into your worksheet.

9. Ctrl + F

Find something specific on your sheet. Think of it as Excel's search engine.

10. Ctrl + H

Replace text or data with a different value. It's like a find-and-replace party.

11. Ctrl + A

Select everything in your current worksheet. You're the master of selection!

12. Ctrl + B

Bold the selected text. Make it stand out like a boss.

13. Ctrl + I

Italicize the selected text. Give it a stylish twist.

14. Ctrl + U

Underline the selected text. Add importance to your words.

15. Ctrl + P

Print your worksheet and bring it to life on paper.

16. Ctrl + W

Close the current workbook and take a break.

17. Ctrl + Tab

Switch between open workbooks with ease.

18. Ctrl + Shift + $

Apply currency formatting to selected cells. Cha-ching!

19. Ctrl + Shift + %

Convert selected cells to percentage format. Show those proportions!

20. Ctrl + Shift + !

Apply number formatting with two decimal places. Keep things precise.

21. Ctrl + Shift +

Apply date formatting to selected cells. Keep track of the time.

22. Ctrl + Shift + @

Apply time formatting to selected cells. Time is of the essence.

23. Ctrl + Shift + * (asterisk)

Select the current region around the active cell. Be the region master!

24. Ctrl + Shift + : (colon)

Enter the current time in the selected cell. Record the moment.

25. Ctrl + Shift + " (quotation mark)

Copy the formula from the cell above. Work smarter, not harder.

26. Ctrl + Shift + + (plus)

Insert cells, rows, or columns with grace.

27. Ctrl + - (minus)

Delete cells, rows, or columns like a pro.

28. Ctrl + Home

Navigate to cell A1. Return to the beginning.

29. Ctrl + End

Navigate to the last cell with data. Reach the end of the line.

30. Ctrl + Page Up

Switch to the previous sheet in your workbook. Time travel, Excel style.

31. Ctrl + Page Down

Switch to the next sheet in your workbook. Keep moving forward.

32. Ctrl + Arrow Keys

Move the active cell in the respective direction without scrolling. Glide through your sheet.

33. Ctrl + Space

Select an entire column in one swift move. Be column-wise.

34. Shift + Space

Select an entire row with elegance. Be row-wise.

35. Alt + = (equal sign)

AutoSum selected cells. Let Excel do the math.

36. Alt + Shift + F1

Insert a new worksheet. Expand your Excel empire.

37. Alt + F4

Close Excel and bid it farewell. Until we meet again.

38. F1

Open Excel Help and seek guidance from the Excel gods.

39. F2

Edit the active cell and start typing. Take control of your data.

40. F4

Repeat the last action. Excel knows you're a creature of habit.

41. F5

Go to a specific cell or range. Excel is your GPS.

42. F9

Calculate all worksheets in all open workbooks. Summon the power of calculation!

43. F11

Create a new chart with one click. Visualize your data.

44. Shift + F11

Insert a new worksheet. Expand your Excel empire.

45. Ctrl + Shift + F3

Create names from row and column labels. Name your data like a pro.

46. Ctrl + Shift + F6

Switch to the previous workbook window. Multitasking is made easy.

47. Ctrl + Shift + F9

Calculate the active worksheet. Let Excel do its magic.

48. Ctrl + Shift + F11

Insert a new worksheet. Expand your Excel empire.

49. Ctrl + Shift + F12

Save the current workbook. Preserve your Excel masterpiece.

50. Alt

Display the shortcut keys for Excel's ribbon commands. Unleash the power of shortcuts.

Conclusion

In conclusion, Excel for Beginners is a powerful tool that can revolutionize the way you handle data and streamline your work processes. It provides a user-friendly interface and a wide range of features that cater to both basic and advanced users. By mastering the fundamentals of Excel, you can efficiently manage and analyze data, create visually appealing charts and graphs, and make informed decisions based on accurate information.

With its versatility and widespread use across various industries, Excel has become an indispensable skill in today's digital world. By embarking on this journey to learn Excel, you have taken a significant step towards enhancing your productivity and boosting your career prospects.

Remember, learning Excel is a continuous process. As you progress, keep exploring new features, experimenting with different functions, and challenging yourself with complex tasks. The more you practice and apply your knowledge, the more proficient you will become.

So do not fear the complexities of Excel, for with dedication and perseverance, you can navigate this vast realm of spreadsheets and data manipulation. Excel for Beginners is just the first step on your journey to harnessing the full potential of this remarkable software.

In closing, embrace the power of Excel and let it become your trusted companion in your professional endeavors. May your data be accurate, your formulas be error-free, and your insights be limitless. Happy Excel-ing!

END

Thank you for reading my book.

Adam K. Grubb

www.ingramcontent.com/pod-product-compliance
Lightning Source LLC
LaVergne TN
LVHW051242050326
832903LV00028B/2531